Collected Poems

Also by Elizabeth Carlson:

To Deliver Me of My Dreams

Collected Poems

Elizabeth Carlson

QUINTESSENTIAL PUBLISHING

SANTA ROSA, CALIFORNIA

Edited by Kathleen Kraemer and the Quintessentials:
Jennifer Mann, Sharon Rivkin, Suzy Stewart, and Joyce Griffin
Design and composition by Wilsted & Taylor, Oakland, California

COVER: Ceramic plate by Sherry Van Gelder

Library of Congress Number: 00-191820   ISBN 0-9703097-0-8

Quintessential Publishing 309 Benton Street, Santa Rosa, California 95401

Additional copies can be purchased through the publisher. Information regarding
the author or publication may also be obtained from the Santa Rosa Junior College
Foundation Office, 1501 Mendocino Avenue, Santa Rosa, California, 95401

She has cast off her body
　　like clothing she no longer needs.
She is turning into spirit, into light.

Contents

Imperfection

I am falling in love
    with my imperfections
The way I never get the sink really clean,
forget to check my oil,
lose my car in parking lots,
miss appointments I have written down,
am just a little late.

I am learning to love
    the small bumps on my face
    the big bump of my nose,
    my hairless scalp,
chipped nail polish,
toes that overlap.
Learning to love
    the open-ended mystery
        of not knowing why

I am learning to fail
    to make lists,
    use my time wisely,
    read the books I should.

Instead I practice inconsistency,
    irrationality, forgetfulness.

Probably I should
hang my clothes neatly in the closet
all the shirts together, then the pants,
send Christmas cards, or better yet
a letter telling of
    my perfect family

But I'd rather waste time
listening to the rain,
or lying underneath my cat
        learning to purr.

I used to fill every empty moment
        with something I could
                cross off later.

Perfect was
        the laundry done and folded
        all my papers graded
        the whole truth and nothing   but

Now the empty mind is what I seek
        the formless shape
                the strange   off center
                sometimes fictional
                                me

                                January 13, 1999

Ordinary Words

These are ordinary words.
They do not startle, terrify, or strike
    through the heart of beauty.
They walk softly across the page
    bewildered, fumbling for the edge
Struggling for a reason.

Broken into shards,
  would they reassemble themselves,
    find a way to become whole,
     walk through fire to live?

Sometimes before I am awake,
    dreams write themselves on paper,
    lovelier than any song,
But in the daylight I am almost mute,
  Longing for what is just
    beneath my skintight mind.

March 19, 1995

when you are gone

when you are gone
        I spread out
fill the   whole house
            with movement, sound.

    do everything at once
            gobbling time as if it were
            going to be rationed tomorrow

stay up late
        not wanting to miss out on a
                single minute,

fall into bed exhausted
        still wanting to read
    or write
            one
                    more

                word.

                        November 28, 1995

4

Ode to Flo

When I see you
    shoot
        straight up
           and out
Accelerating swiftly
    to the front
        of any race you run
Hair flying,
    body molded
        to its quest
Of ever greater speed and ease,

I find that place
    inside myself
Where beauty lives and breathes,
That racehorse
    in the blood and bones
That knows the way
    to my own finish line —

The fastest woman in the world.

The miracle is not
    that you should run so fast
        or be so beautiful
           or strong,
But that we want it that way,
Want a woman to be fast and beautiful and strong
And–yes–black.

The gold belongs to every girl
Who ever thought that dark skin was a blemish,

Curly hair a curse
Or a mind a thing to hide.

You rise
        out of the ashes
                    of our dreams
And flowing, glowing,
        teach us
                how to fly.

September 28, 1988

Homeboy

Oh yeah—
Manny's got a grip.
Bought a condo
ten years after
it was hip.
Too small for guests
so they stay at his website
(www.home)
curl up next to the picture
of him and his cat,
baseball hats on backwards
mugging for the camera.

Manny takes ballroom,
hoping to score.
Knows salsa, twostep,
western swing
but the tango
eludes him.

We go for coffee,
catch up.
I tell him,
Hang in there, bro.
He show me pics
from his last vacation.
Club Med, Tahiti.
Cute chicks with tans
fooling around with his muscle.
He never got
their phone numbers.

Saw Manny last week
at the Marina Safeway
buying organic greens and shrimp.
Trying to impress
some new lady.
I tell him,
Go for it.
Help him pick out the wine.
We go way back.

February 16, 1998

For Sarah at Eight

Out of the flower
    the seed
out of the seed
    the flower.

Birthing itself over and over
    suspended between heaven
        and earth
    between holding on
        and letting go
    the umbilical cord still throbbing
        between us.

Longing to enfold you
    as I once did with my
        large body
    my belly keeping you safe
        or so it seemed
    from the world's insanity,
I would again make a greenhouse of my love
    for you to flower
        unmolested
    into your own sweet bloom of being.

From the moment we met,
    we were parted.

Birth is the first goodbye—
    the seed leaving the flower,
        beginning the flower.

1985

All-American Girls

*for the women of the All-American Professional
Girls Baseball League, 1943–1954*

"Look like women—play like men!"
he said
And so they did,
in dresses cut to show
the curve of thigh and calf.
Sliding into base,
      they scraped the skin off
      those same legs
      that had been thought
too tender for the sport,
And hit an ever smaller, harder ball
beyond the wildest dreams
of all the avaricious, sleazy men
      who thought they had created them,
Endured the catcalls
passing for flirtation
      from guys who couldn't catch
      the drift
Of their least, lazy, looping fly,
While they played every day
and sometimes twice
in heat and wind and rain.
The pure delight of movement
was enough to pay
for endless bus rides,
bad food,
the disappearance
of the men
they might have married.

Eleven years it lasted,
an enchanted diamond of time.
The men off somewhere
killing each other again,
The women suddenly released
from baking, sewing, milking, cleaning—
Free to swing a bat, to crush a ball,
To run until their sides ached,
> To slide headlong into the waiting base,
> > To knock each other down,
To feel the joy of reaching,
> the smack of ball in glove,
the fine, firm filament of their alliance—
> connection forged in peaceful combat.

They called the names of their brief sisterhood—
Chicks, Redwings, Peaches, Belles. . . . .
Their muscles sang
against their skirts
and they became
> Wood, leather, earth, air, fire. . . . .

Transformed, they slipped,
> Houdini-like, invisible,
out of the bondage
> of male fantasy,
> and found their own
sweet childhood dream,
The ecstasy of play.

July, 1992

Maine Morning

Up at first light
        like a child on Christmas morning
     rushing downstairs
       to see what gifts
          await me —

Sunlight,
       birdsong
          clear, flowing water,
      silence

interspersed with hammering
    as humans construct their nests

I want to memorize this place,
  take it home with me
       wrapped carefully
       like the shells and driftwood
           in my suitcase
to spread out
       on a grey California morning
when there is no water
       in sight.

July 3, 1992

Gardening in June in Connecticut

My fingers dig into soil made rich by years of living.
The waste I cursed before, plowed back
    becomes a sacred gift,
    lines my fingernails with juicy hope.

I wear a hat to shield me
    from rain falling on my seedling hair
    and wonder what will flower
    from these random seeds into this sheltered air.

A city girl, my childhood plants
    were radishes and carrots in a cup
    nurtured on a fire escape,
    not meant for eating, though I often
    pulled them up to look.

Now, in my country home so far from here
    I never plant or harvest
    since the deer ate it all
    that first year.

But in this quiet space,
    with images of God around me everywhere,
    my newfound seeds may germinate—who knows?
    become a mixed bouquet not seen before.

My pen the spade that turns the dark loam over,
    sifting through the layers that surround my heart
    pointing softly to its beating core.

Villa Maria
June 16, 1998

Found Poetry

Fumbling around
    in a cluttered purse,
I came upon a piece of crumpled paper,
      yellow, lined,
        looking like an old shopping list.

Something I must have
        scribbled to myself
while waiting in line at the bank
    or in a doctor's office
    stripped naked
      on that cold table
        with a draft sneaking up the opened back
    of my paper smock.

The ink was smeared
    and it didn't even look like
      my handwriting
but the words fell off the page
    and tumbled back
      into my waiting heart

      reminding me that
a poem is merely
    the shape of the lump in your throat,
      the missed heart beat
      alchemized.

July 27, 1992

Empty

They had taken it
    all out of her
        while she slept—

A daylight robbery
    (with her permission, of course)
never one to object
    if it was reasonable or fair
        or would help the greater good
    or if it could be shown
      that she would be none the worse for it
        afterwards.

She is not quite sure
    if the empty space inside her
is something she can feel—
    a stomach wanting food—
or if it is all in her mind,
    this womblessness
    this basket emptied of its eggs
      unhatched.

Don't count them,
    they always said.
Don't count them.

May 9, 1994

15

The Closet

The shape of my closet is
square. It has no windows.
The air is thick. I sit behind the
coats, hunched over. My knees
drawn up. Scarves float
above my head. The tap
slap of a branch
can almost be heard. Inside
it is warm and dark. I listen for
an invitation to emerge. None comes.
If I am to leave, it appears
it will be up to me. I fall
asleep dreaming of the open space
outside.

March 25, 1995

Alpine Morning

No blinds on the windows.
I want the sun to startle me awake,
call me out to see this scoop of valley,
carpeted with yellow and purple,
aspen leaves shimmering like silent wind chimes,
the shadowed peaks of mountains
reminding me of winter with their still snowy
patches, the dangerous air
alive in its transparent richness.

Breathing it in, I feel my body
lighten, float above the ground,
conjure images of Heidi, waking at dawn,
peering through the round loft window
anticipating cheese and milk,
the romp through the meadow with the goats,
and grandfather, stern and loving,
making it safe to be a child again.

Bear Valley
August 12, 1995

Lizzie

She stands
    at the top of the slide,
holding on
    to the round railing,
anticipating
    the sweet release
        of downward motion,
almost out of control,
    the swift metal
        not quite burning her thighs.

She swings
    head tilted back
        to absorb the trees,
     her legs rowing the air
        creating her own motion
feeling the heart stopping thrill
    in her stomach,
        between her pumping legs.
The swing flying out so far, so high
    until it orbits the park.
Herself a floating planet
    a meteor, not yet fallen
        to earth.

She walks
    balancing along the wire fences
     arms outstretched.
    Her mind is somewhere else,
        creating stories
The Brooklyn street
    becomes a prairie

        beckoning a covered wagon,
the park, a mysterious wood.

Her body seems to grow
      elastic
    lengthening like shadows.

She plays
    throwing the ball against the stoop
      over and over. . . .
The firm, smooth, round resilience of it
      is a joy.

She jumps through
    boxes drawn with chalk
      and hides
        and seeks
          and hides
            and seeks again. . . . .

July 29, 1992

Poetic Potion

Brooklyn dust,
     grass growing through pavement
sound of a ball hitting a stoop,
     the gold that shines in the leaves in the twilight,
the music of rain
     shapes emerging out of fog,
the hush of the first snowstorm.

Ice crystals
     clicking in the trees
Little House stories
     playing out on the staircase,
dressup clothes
     and the curtain going up,
toe shoes still unworn.

The sound of a cello playing alone
ocean's deep heartbeat,
     the essence of foam
bread baking in a sunlit kitchen
     and the stars
stretched above everything
     waiting, infinite. . . . . .

Sweet Home Chicago

Tall buildings jeweled, light-filled
    thrusting into a cold sky.

Blues belted out
    the air full of notes
The three hundred pound cab driver rocking
    to his own beat

Squashed into a corner
    with Canadians, southerners, Nebraskans
      locals, black and white

The room fills with the joy
    of shared heartbreak.
We pound and stomp and scream.
Our religion is sweat and music played
    straight from the soul—
Kid Dynamite struts, becomes James Brown
    the king of soul
We fall in love with a man the size of a child.

"I've reached a turning point in my life"
    he sings
and I have. I know I'm not going home
the same.

October 28, 1995

Dog Food

He was fifteen years old,
locked up, waiting
to find out
if he would be found
fit
to be tried
as a child
for an armed robbery
where someone died.

He stole cars
because he liked to drive.
Eight in one night once.
Drove them till he ran
out of gas, then found
another.

Abandoned
by his addict mother,
raised in foster homes.
Once he was allowed
a pet, a pit
bull. He named it Mommy.

His friends called him
Dog Food.

Adult or child?
You tell me.

January 16, 1996

Pain Drives Out Everything

This poem I am trying to write
the beauty of this never to be lived again
spring day in the desert
bougainvillea sweetness of the air
naptime dreams
taste of an orange
desire to do anything.

My spirit feels as if
it has been shoved into a small airless
corner of my being.

Body takes over.
Body is all
and body can find no safe good place,
wishes for oblivion.
Spirit can barely remember
a day spent with energy,
without pain.

A day of paying attention to
the world
 always alive
          breathing my name.

                              April 29, 1998

Remembering: Mario and Anne

He died this month, his age the same as mine

                      She died the year after I was born

He spoke liquid fire

          She wrote rough diamonds, called through barbed wire

We were not related

                      They were not related

Except in the pure flame of spirit

                      Except in innocence galvanized

He shunned the limelight, it followed him anyway

            She longed for fame, didn't know it would come

He was called to speak

                      She wrote in hiding

    Surrounded by many

                    Protected by few

He warned of coming danger

                She believed in goodness, in hope

    In speech, freedom

                    In writing, immortality

            Unlikely heroes

          alive to their moment

             not dead

             not yet

                      November 23, 1996

Jilly Leaving

She drives straight
        up and out
Her brand new shiny car
        (named for the planet
                of limitation)
Crammed full
        of possibility and possession —

Lamps, stereo, books, shoes,
        the James Dean poster leaning
                against the stuffed bunny —

A lifetime of memories,
        of growth
Surround and cradle her
        as she takes
                these first new steps,
        not wobbly, as in the babyhood
                I never saw,
        but strong, determined.

The second grade has a new teacher.
And this still little girl,
        who used to drink in tales
                of Narnia and Nancy Drew
                        and every Little House adventure,
        sets forth
                in her own covered wagon,
        the road opening before her,
                an unfolding story.

The horn honks briefly
at the top of the driveway,
announcing her flight,
her arrival.

July 1, 1993

Special Delivery

You never know when
a poem will come hurtling
mysteriously through space
to land at your feet,
an unopened parcel
not necessarily addressed to you.
It ticks warningly. Is it a bomb
or just a beating heart?

Take courage.
Open it.
If it explodes in your face, if
your hands are separated forever
from your arms, if blood
spatters on the page,
at least you haven't died
quietly,
for nothing.

October 27, 1995

Dancing at the Pub

We take over the bar
    push the chairs to the side of the room,
        fill the juke box with songs we can dance to—

Santana, Phil Collins, the Beatles, the Stones

In front of the dart board
    we dance uncoupled,
        flinging our bodies against the beat
            finding ways to flow
        around and through each other,
freed from chairs, from thinking, from
        the tyranny of time.

A thin film of sweat connects us,
    overflows our borders,
        runs down our faces
            into our beer.

Go girl! Work it!

The locals don't know what to make of us.
Women dancing with women, men with men.
Soon they too are looped in.
    "Awesome," one drunk guy repeats
            again and again.

As we slip off our degrees
    and any hint of discipline,
    riding the rhythm,
        we bump and grind—
        an ecstasy of inclusion.

Midnight catches up with us.
We close the place down
    walk home arm in arm
       under more stars
           than there are in the States,
      looking for true North together.

The night air enfolds us,
      calls us friend.

Potlatch '95

Guilt

Guilt sits
    like a sharp-clawed
    bird upon my shoulder
Rasping in my ear,
  its pointed talons
    digging ever deeper
    drawing blood
Its voice a constant
  whisper, jabber, drone—
"I will never leave you,
    never leave you."
It mocks
    my own faithful vow.

I bring it offerings
  of raw meat
    pieces of my heart
    fresh-killed.
It eats, but it is not
    satisfied.
At night it haunts me
    Shadowlike
It flies about the room.
Waking I find it
    perching, watchful
      by my bed.
Even in dreams
    I feel the cold
      brush of its feathers
Its wingspread
  hides the sun.

It loves to feed
     upon my happiness
Picking the joy upon my tongue
     to bitter dust
Leaving my mouth
     empty of words,
      my heart
        closed to comfort.

January 15, 1989

Montana & Lily at the Coast

She lets us off the leash here.
We stick close by.
Except when a hawk dips down
I can't resist the urge to chase it.
She thinks I think I'll catch it
but I know better.
It's just an excuse to run
and the graceful arc of its wings
helps lift me, moves me faster
as if I'm flying too.
I leave the earth each instant
returning lighter than I went.
The air blows my ears back
and I can hear for miles,
smell every dog that ever ran here.

Lily checks the rocks, the holes,
finds the watery places where we drink.
She's the older, wiser dog or so they say.
I love her like a sister.
She bites me sometimes to keep me in line.
Or when she's jealous.
I don't mind.
I would rather have her nagging company
than be alone.
Here on the ridge we're the same age.
We sniff the same tufts of grass,
lie down in the sun together,
wait for this woman we love
to decide it's time to go.

We're used to having no control
over when
or if.

January 9, 1997

Meditation

I walk
   down

one
   exhale
        at
       a
         time

to the center
   of my   self

the place
    of no secrets

the wide expanse
    of everything
    and nothing

to explain

to make right

to do over.

      Breathing is all

I have
     to do

I am perfect
at it

always.

April 9, 1999

Morning, November

We wake in the dark.
I bring the steaming cups
of coffee. We hold them
reverentially, the warmth translating
itself through our hands
before the smoky elixir
finds its way inside. The dog places
his silky head in your lap.
You scratch his ears. I ruffle your hair.
We do not speak.

Words present themselves.
I finger them lovingly, turning
each over in my mind
like a smooth stone,
admiring its structure and resonance —
encantatory, cavernous,
forlorn —

Each one miraculous, newborn
in the silent morning,
like the day itself —
untried, yet still
vibrating.

November 30, 1995

Three Poems for Dayle

A night full of fireworks
illuminates the ordinary
miracle of life on earth—
the quiet snore of a dog underfoot
a baby burping
fog rolling its wet caress
over every blade of grass
smoke lifting from a fire,
carrying the faintest trace
of memory along the path
to the sea,
and you always there waiting
at the end of the day,
waiting for me.

II

You lie next to me, your warm
breath filling my ears, your arm
heavy across my shoulder, hand
cupping my breast.
I move my hips against you,
but you do not awaken.
Your head rests on my hair,
pulling it at the roots when I move.
Still I love the sweet heaviness of you,
the warm comfort of your holding me,
making sure I don't fly
all to pieces in the night.

III

they laugh in the kitchen while
she stirs the chicken in the sauce and
he eats yogurt from a carton
pushing the spoon into her mouth
brushing his leg against her hip
as she loads the dishwasher
sparks fly between them
the house swims around this small space
they inhabit together.
a thin thread connects the kitchen
to the bedroom. they wind it up
and fall into the warm cocoon
of their embrace

December 31, 1995

Virgin, Mother, Crone

for Jill

Just as the moon transforms from one phase to another, the Great Goddess
moves among her many roles. Her three faces are usually virgin, mother,
and crone: virgin representing the strong, self-defined goddess; mother
representing the nurturing goddess . . . and crone representing the goddess
of death and transformation. The Triple Goddess reminds us of our
sacredness regardless of our age or function in life.

MICHAEL BABCOCK, *Susan Boulet Goddesses Knowledge Cards*

You were virgin.
     I, not quite mother, but wanting to be.

You nudged me there, quietly,
     your alert brown eyes
     trusting me slowly.

Soon I couldn't imagine
     life without you or your sister in it.
Soon I couldn't imagine not
     adding another of my own.

Now there is one more virgin
     starting her road,
     with you her guide, her nurturing source.
Your roundness emptying gracefully
     into the perfection
        of Emily Elizabeth.

One week old today.
All her adventures but one in front of her.

I move to the grandmother chair,
 reach out gratefully to hold her,
  to add whatever wisdom may have
   accidentally touched me in these years.

        Grandma Liz
        October 16, 1998

Waiting for Her

Light seeps under the blinds,
pries apart your eyelids
like an envelope steamed carefully open.
The clock glows, an altar
in the darkened room. Outside
car sounds multiply.
You hallucinate her return—
imagine the sound of a radio
played too loud, a slamming door,
feet running down the walkway,
the dogs barking their annoying greeting.
Firecrackers, sirens, the squeal of brakes—
a thousand calamities suggest themselves
against the neutral backdrop of night.
Nothing is as vulnerable
as your only child loose in the world
unless it is your heart.

July 4, 1995

Excavation

Open the door, she said,
    and walk through
to rooms filled with feelings,
    the chairs stuffed silly with
        chances to take.

Only pull off the frozen doilies,
    find the hidden treasure
        underneath.

Can you imagine
    what might be waiting
after all this time
    if you could just break through
        to China
    standing on your head
      and not worry about
    if any of it made sense?

April 14, 1995

The Audience

There was always someone watching
   as she got up in the morning,
      ate Rice Krispies,
      fought with her little sister,
      played in the park,
      touched herself under the covers

   as her parents argued
      or hugged or lectured
and her grandmother stood
        in the kitchen,
          owning it.

The walls became transparent,
      the roof came off
   and the light trained itself
      upon whoever was speaking,
        their words suddenly important,
        their gestures grown larger,
          dramatic.

Quietly, the invisible audience
      sat watching,
      their breathing imperceptible
      except to the hairs on the end of her arm
        standing upright,
      except to her heart,
        thumping with the excitement of it,
          her life emerging out of shadow,
           becoming real.

August 20, 1994

43

Reconstructive Surgery

First they take away
your breast.
The one that could kill you.
Cells multiplying put
of control. Too much life equals
death in this case.
You have to go
along with it. What else
can you do? The scar remains
where once your lover cupped
the soft fullness of your body.
The other breast sags sweetly,
accusing in its perfection.

You are unbalanced.
Every day you put on a
disguise beneath your clothes.
A one-breasted woman looks
funny. There is no way
around it.

You wait. The time passes.
The cells behave themselves.
You want that breast back—
or a reasonable facsimile.
You are sick to death
of being lopsided. It is natural
to want two. And it can be done.
So they carve it
out of your stomach, your thigh,
wait for tissue to declare itself
with you or against you,

build you a new one, sew on a
nipple. Like the dolls we used
to make out of stockings, only so much
more anatomically correct.

Amazing what they can do
these days. Your clothes look good now.
You pass for whole.

January 19, 1996

Pupa

She hangs
     upside down
     inside her self-created shell
patient, gestating
feeling a quiet rumbling
     like gas
          or the shift of tectonic plates
         or the soft kicking
         of baby feet.
The wings form themselves,
     the colors deepen
         in the darkness.
There will be no labor pains this time
     when the soul flies free.

May 16, 1994

Running Away From Home

Sometimes she lets herself
        imagine it.
The morning newborn,
        her car waiting, silent
                in the driveway.

A cup of coffee to go
        and no note.
Just a vase of fresh picked flowers
        to remind them.

The highway opens up,
        the white line a conveyor belt
                moving her forward.

She always goes north,
  the ocean on her left,
    stops briefly for a sandwich
        and a devilled egg, maybe
            ice cream in the afternoon.

Nights she stays in little inns,
        the ocean a mantra,
                the soundtrack to her movie.

Where she ends up
        is never important.
Only that it is a place to begin all over
                as if you could get younger that way.

She pictures herself waiting tables.
"What'll you have, hon?" she says
    a pencil tucked behind her ear.

Trucks rumble by outside.
The drivers rest for a moment.
    The meal is always breakfast.

August 3, 1996

Margot Frank

No one ever tells the other story
        of the other sister

oldest child, serious and plain
      depressed, afraid

She was the one the Germans wanted first
Her name was on the orders

Sending them quickly into hiding
      that July day

She kept no diary, lived in silence
      like most of us

What did she think of
      in those long hours of waiting

The cramped rooms
      the shrunken life of hiding

At night on her unfolded cot
      did the breathing of her family comfort or smother her

Did she dream of dances, of beaux
      a life she should have led

Did she love or hate her little sister

No pen appeared
    to tempt her toward immortality

No one writes
    her unknown story down.

                November 23, 1996

A Dream of Vietnam

I am entering a tunnel
wearing combat fatigues.
Strapped to my back, a pack,
a gun.
There is no way out.
No appeal to gender
or conscience. I must kill
or be killed, watch others die.

A short Vietnamese man
is my guide. He greets me
at the entrance to the cave,
forces me to look back—
the sight forbidden Orpheus, Lot's Wife—
at what I am leaving behind.
The evening houses sharp and
enduring in their familiarity.
The sky streaked pink behind
them. Every kind of weather
possible. Never has the world
looked so beautiful as in this moment
of leaving.

He tells me, "Remember this place.
It could save your life someday."
Tells me how it saved his
when his Chinese captors let down
their guard and he found
his way back.

I promise to remember,
turning toward the tunnel,
the waiting horror.

January 19, 1996

Power Outage, Tuesday 2 p.m.

Fingers poised to enter the next circle
    in the slinky descent into
        Internet hell,

The lights go out
    and I find myself
        in the procrastinator's dark night of the
            soul.

Compelled to write poems
    with pen and ink
        by candlelight,

I daydream of a mermaid
    whose glowing hair illuminates the lake
    on which she rows me
        to the nearer shore.

I tie my boat to any tree.
    The forest flares beside my silent skin.
    Glowworms flicker in the fading light.

The phone rings
    and my heart beats back to life.

I lose the dream dreaming me.

December 27, 1994

At a Dorothea Lange Exhibit

I

MIGRANT MOTHER, NIPOMO, 1936

"The crop froze this year and the family
is destitute. On this morning they had sold the tires of
their cars to pay for food. She is 32 years old."

You nurse with what milk?
      No food to give the older one
          who leans against your shoulder.
Your brow furrows with
      the long worry of it,
          the no end in sight.

In the gallery, heels click against
      marble floors.
A young mother,
      her baby round and well fed,
    stares into your eyes
      as if to share her milk
        with you.

Two well dressed women smile, remembering.
"I always felt so peaceful
      after I nursed," one says,
          ignoring your exhausted frown.

They cannot see,
      for all your pointing
         to the truth.

II
TO DOROTHEA

You did not need to do
    anything
  but point your camera,
   train the lens
     on the misery, the dignity
       of the poor.

The people did the rest.

Like the woman of the High Texas Plains,
    right hand clapped
      across her forehead,
   left hand cradling her thin neck,
     regretting the loss of the car
        that could have taken her away
         from there—
   sold for beans,
     to eat, to heat, to survive—
      no beanstalk magic to a promised land—

Or the argument
    in a Richmond trailer camp
 a man and woman, lovers once,
        poverty stripping their bed bare.

Or the Japanese families,
    tags on their clothing
      like so much baggage, waiting
       to be shipped—
their sons in uniform to fight for Uncle Sam.

You made us look at what we didn't want to see,
　make us look now
　　　at the man lying filthy
　　　　in the doorway
　　　at the lines leading to no work,
　　　　　　no food, no shelter.

The technicolor version of
　　　your black and white essay
　　　　　waits outside the museum door
where a man asks me for spare change.
　and still I pass him by.

When will the photograph burn through the page
　　　enough to change
　　　　　his life, my life?

August 16, 1994

Survivors

I do not wish to know what
      you have come to tell us,
  what you have borne with your flesh,
        endured in the relentless returning of dreams,
          hearing the heartbeats always of the others —

      the ones who died before they could be liberated,
    who died on the way to the camps,
      or in ghettoes, already hopeless,
    the ones who died from eating the wrong food
      when food was finally there to be eaten,
        wiped out in a plague
    of liberation, like the Indians wrapping themselves in
  blankets laced with smallpox.

I do not want to hear your stories.
You, who look like my mother, my father, my grandmother
 before them,
Who speak still in the accent of the old world.
I avoid your gaze in the ways you tell us you
   were avoided then, the way we avoid meeting the eyes
        of the homeless man in the street, holding the sign.

You keep discreetly covered
        the blue tattoo of numbers that would scare us.
You dole out the words, carefully,
   answer our questions with a thin smile, a cough,
        an economy of truth.

I do not want to know.
I cannot keep from listening.

                     March 14, 1995

Passover, 1995

What does Passover mean to me?
       she asked,
     but it would be too real
        too painful if she only knew
that it meant running
    away from home when I was twenty
    crossing the Red Sea of the Rocky Mountains
       in a silver Porsche
    with the slavecatchers always trailing me,
      trying to catch up
         to bring me home.
I changed my name twice,
    my address several times
Still she came
    charging across the country
  moving coincidentally down the street
She never leaves me alone.
In silent nights
    I escape again
      into dreams, poems
Hide where I can in
    bushes, branches, buried in the sand.
She sniffs me out.
How could I have dared to think
  I was a protected witness
    with a new ID?
They always find you,
    always will until
You are willing to stand naked on the scaffold
    in the harsh sun of noon
with nothing to hide anymore.

                    April 14, 1995

Sanctuary

Remembering yesterday— the
bright air, fragrance of wildflowers—
lupine, forget-me-not, Indian paintbrush,
wild mint, sage, the plant we call lambs ears
that the Indians used to staunch wounds,
snow reaching down to meadowland,
pine cones crunching underfoot,
the trail appearing, then hiding again
leaving rock and snow to thread our way
across.

Music suddenly fills the air.
The notes float up, obliterate
whatever treacherous thought
might seek to rob me of my peace.
A cure for whatever is wrong
is simply to sit still
in this thin, sun-drenched mountain air
and listen.

August 13, 1995

For Dayle

You sleep in
 On your birthday
A well-deserved rest
  while I try
 to capture on a page
Some essence
 of your being
 elusive as a moth
  fluttering towards the ceiling
  the words won't be trapped
   won't stay
just as you
  won't be pinned
   above a neat conclusion.
Old before
 you had a chance to be young
  and you still refuse to grow up
Your childlike spirit fills the room,
 lifts me out of my despair
You see the worst
 but somehow believe
  the best
Hurt souls flourish under your care.

We have had our dark times,
 voices raised in anger
  and blame,
Yet last night
 in the middle of a sentence
  I felt your hand
   stroking my arm

your eyes
    loving me
        beyond the moment
My foolish words
    went on
but my heart heard,
  my skin absorbed
    your touch.

February 6, 1993

Condemned to Write

You said you were
  condemned to write.
   Forced to sit nightly at a cramped desk
    the words sliding onto the page
     against your will
   serving an indeterminate
    sentence,
the entrances and exits
  multiplying into scenes and acts
the chapters building
  to a novel
   you never intended.

How I wish
  for this same penance—
  to be strapped into
  my chair,
 fed crusts of bread and water only
  until the pages
  fill up with my blood
and the sun becomes the moon
  a thousand times,
 and the cake
  with the file buried in it,
   promise of sweet release,
   turns to mold
    in a corner,
While the muse
  plays through me
   like wind in eucalyptus
broadcasting the scent of creation.

August 1, 1992

Naramata Morning

If there is a heaven,
      I am sure it looks like Naramata.
Flower-filled and bird-blessed,
      the green softness of the shoulders,
    the hips, sloping toward the lake,
         liquid circle
            cradling fish and waterfowl.

Lupine, wild rose, lilac, clover,
      dogs wagging their way down main street,
    the rhythmic swoosh of sprinklers,
        even in the rain.

Here breathing is an act of prayer,
      walking a meditation.

The loon laughs over the lake
        and we human beings
    remember
        who we can become
          who we have always known
        we are.

June 14, 1997

Waking Daydream

In the middle of a lake,
        rowing for dear life,
                the wind pushing against my futile oars
I am rescued
        by a mermaid
                with silky eels for hair
                        and biceps of iron.
She turns the boat around
        and rowing with the wind
                carries me safely to shore.
Her eely hair glows in the dark.
The power has gone out everywhere
        But in my singing heart.

December 27, 1994

In my dreams

In my dreams I don't have cancer
and everyone is younger.
I rush around, trying to please,
as always. Trying to make things right.

My curly hair still billows
around my head
and friends long vanished
reappear, glistening.

Awkward teenage girls
confide in me.
My daughter, still a child,
holds me by the hand.

There is a baby, sleeping
in my bedroom
and nothing
I cannot do.

January 9, 1998

Necessary Angels

Tucked in the corner
of my favorite coffee shop,
imagining myself invisible
beneath my turban,
I feel her approach my table.
Bleached hair cropped short,
face much younger than mine,
her large body easily
taking up its space.
She hopes that she's not making a mistake.
"I was in chemotherapy last year," she says.
"Hang in there."
I ask her if her hair was always blonde,
wonder if I'd have the nerve.
"Honey," she says, "once we've been through this,
we can do anything we want!"

Yoga class. Two weeks in a row
I am paired with the same lovely woman.
Soft eyes, a firm touch.
We gently massage each other's back.
She gives to me first, then I to her.
I don't know her name but I know
the muscle in her back, where the tight places are,
trust her to touch me.
Afterwards she strokes my leg, tells me
"I'm a cancer survivor—two years now."
I want more of her story
but there isn't time for details—
only the telepathy of hope.
We go back to our own mats.
I lie letting her sweetness allow me to cry.

All over town they fly,
wings hidden, hair grown back,
appearing when I most need them.
No payment ever for their grace.

February 19, 1998

Transatlantic Call

You call from Bordeaux,
  your sweet bird voice
 reminding me of all our conversations
   since your birth

First gurgles, then words, sentences and paragraphs
  tumbling, irrepressible.

My own voice scratchy and weak
  tries to meet yours strongly.

No use.

You will have to accept me
    as I am now

  needing you more
    than you need me.

October 6, 1997

68

What the Heart Wants

"The heart wants what it wants"
WOODY ALLEN, 1992

My heart wants
    an open field, a lake,
        a path leading
            deep
        into the woods
My heart wants
    a book with no last page,
        a candle
    burning simply in a dark room
My heart wants
    your heart
        beating where I can feel it
    your warm bearlike embrace
      smoothing the wrinkles underneath my skin
My heart wants
    a window
        facing the ocean
and an endless summer day
    filled with imagination
My heart wants
    to ride horseback
        into country I have never seen
    My heart wants never to have to
        again
My greedy heart
    wants only
        and always
            what it wants. . . . . . .

            August 25, 1992

Music From Bear Valley

Last night in the white tent
I was so close to the second violinist
three rows back that I could see
her almost lose her place, regain it,
the quick fingers picking up the line,
the pizzicato dance of right hand plucking
melody from left. Most eyes were
on the stage, where the Count sang his amorous
advances to Susannah hiding in the closet, on Cherobino
transmogrifying in and out of gender, Figaro
capsizing the count beneath
the weight of his own lechery,
but I was transfixed by the luminous face
of the longhaired concertmaster, carried aloft by
sounds I could almost hear. I folded myself
into the nearest cello, felt the bow
slide across my strings, became the music.
This morning perched above the valley,
the Ode to Joy floating from below,
I find I have arrived in heaven,
where despite my many misdeeds,
the angels sing me welcome.

August 13, 1995

Midnight Dream

When the taxi driver hands you the wheel
in the middle of the intersection
there is nothing to do
but make a U-turn
and try like hell not to get killed
as you search for the address he gave you—
a hotel you used to know,
now pink and purple, run by gays.

A not so gay man is
throwing a fit in the lobby
as you deliver your package,
try to leave.
Suddenly they are putting him
in your backseat, strapping him in.
He is your burden now,
your purpose.

This young man with AIDS,
whose name you don't even know,
has a mother
worrying about him
through the long night,
has a lover
somewhere
maybe.

The stars bear witness
to your strange journey,
        your new path, unchosen,
                inescapable.

You wake up shivering,
understanding too much
of what it means.

April 25, 1995

Lilyusha

Once you leaped high
        across a Moscow backdrop,
                no limits to your reach, your
                        stretch, your longing for just one more
                                inch of life.

Your daughter leaps
        across a different photograph,
                the long line of leg
                        tracing the shoreline,
                the curve of her back
                        important as the ocean, the sun . . .

Now you live inside.
Your body collapsed
        into its snail-like shell.
Tiny and shuffling, you roam your small terrain.

Hand in hand, we wander
        the museum of your home.
You, who lived in theatres, studios, cafes,
        on beaches, in the air, leaping . . .

Now your hand shakes
        as you pour the tea,
                but pour it out you will.
No matter that a few drops spill.

She was your bird in flight,
                your life made whole.
    Of all your fledgling students,

she alone
      carried your spirit into space.

There is no justice in a universe
      that stops such beauty in midflight,
           and sentences you, imprisoned in your pain, to life.

                                   December 29, 1994

Don't Waste Your Time

Don't waste your time on earth
doing the work of others.
Do your own work.
The sweat of your soul,

The lightness in the center of your heart
will tell you
when you are on course.

The swiftness of your breath
will slow to match
the tidal pull of moonlight.

You will ski effortlessly
down the slope of each day
calling your own name
softly to the trees.

December 18, 1997

Arch Rock, August 28

All day I felt it pull me
    until I had to go,
        wound toward it like a fish
        reeled in,
    my face slapped windy on the hillside,

Around and through the opening
    made by its own fluid force
        the foam-tipped ocean swirls,
    the rock dissolves,
        becomes a gateway
            to the sea beyond.

Sixteen years ago today
    I held the image of this rock
        with my inner eye,
    the pain of each contraction
        seizing my body,
            inviting it to tense against
                the tidal pull of birth.

Around and through,
    contractions swirling
 vision of water pushing through stone
    allowing the firm container of my womb
        to transform itself
        into a channel

    through which you came,
        intrepid journeyer,
          fighting, flowing
            swimming toward the light.

August 28, 1993

Leaving You There

It was hard enough.
The van empty, like the cast-off years of your life,
    the empty nest dragged home behind us,
       our tears alternating
          remembering together how you used to be,
         driving towards a life suddenly
          cleaned up, boring.

But that image of you falling backwards,
    your eyes fluttering closed like
    a living china doll
    as you leaned into the floor of your dorm room,
       groaning, unconscious,
         wouldn't leave me alone.

I reach out to catch you
    but you fall again and again through my not quite
    reaching arms,
    hit your head hard on the floor,
    wake up confused, disoriented.

Then the emergency room.
    I hold your hand,
       your head rests on my shoulder.
         You are pale, subdued.
    I tell you stories of all the times I fainted,
       hate myself for almost enjoying this moment,
         this reprieve from leaving.

What is the point of all this mothering
    if they only leave you alone?

if they can fall backwards standing right next to you
        and you can't even catch them?

You sleep in a new bed now—one I never chose for you.
Your view of palm trees and tennis courts,
      so different from our hill of evergreens,
         the creek in the canyon, solitude.
Your neighbors, a noisy floor of youth
    arranged by twos and fours.

We wander around an all too quiet house,
      the rooms reverberating with your absence,
         looking for you everywhere.

September 30, 1995

Colette Goes to Costco

I used to be afraid to come here by myself—
the looming cartons, huge box-movers,
carts like flatbed trucks and equally
enormous people pushing into line with
years' supplies of Pampers, soapflakes, beer;
the noise of commerce to the nineteenth power
making a mockery of anyone
who only needs one tube of toothpaste or a cake of soap
to wash the moment clean. But now I love
the eclectic jumble—books and ice cream, film and magic markers
by the gross. Tasting free samples,
I eat my way down cavernous aisles, buy more
than I need or can pile into my tiny car,
Colette's novels and a mammoth jar
of sundried tomatoes sitting companionably
with toilet paper in my cart.

May 26, 1995

Java Point, 3 p.m.

Just before the midafternoon rush,
I take my decaf mocha to a window
table, bordered by books, the once
or twice read mysteries of other vacations,
soak up the local ambience of tourists
mixed with those who call this piece of coast
their home, have found a way to eke a living from
this soil of bookstores, galleries, gourmet cafes,
carpentry, massage and fishing boats,
where every other person is a realtor.

And what is real here but the swish of surf,
the call of gulls, the endless reassuring tide
that pulls us all no matter how far inland
we have strayed. Here on this northern California
coast we gather like nesting cormorants, pulling our
food from the sea, leaving our waste a decoration
on the rocks, proclaiming our good fortune.

At the Union 76

Waiting to use the pump, I find myself
staring at the lower leg and foot
of a woman one bay over,
hanging out the passenger window
of a Chevy Nova, circa 1980, bashed in front fender,
chains attached to the rear trailer hitch,
paint peeling off its scratched and dented
burgundy surface. Her old man in surfer pants and sleeveless tee,
hair pulled back in a pony tail, fills the tank from the rear
as she lolls or lies dead in the front seat. I cannot see her face which
may be ugly, pock-marked, full of acne and despair.
Still her graceful calf leans out the window, painted
toenails sexy,   arch of foot beckoning,
resting softly on the air.

May 26, 1995

Cruisin' with A.

Desert stars glow cold
    Above the asphalt
Top down, heater turned up high
    He in black leather,
        I in borrowed warmth
Riding, jiving
    To the barrio beat
        Of Los Lobos
Loud as we can stand it
    On the Avis stereo

Night air crisp and purging
Blows away the plastic dust
    that settles in the hotel rooms
        and golf courses
            and minds of those who drink
            at this oasis.

Prematurely white hair gleaming, glowing
    in reflected street moonlight,
He regales me with tales
    of A. A. meetings
        peopled with tattooed lowlife
          instead of stars
Not what you'd expect
    in Palm Springs in November.

We escape
    for just a moment.

Wheelchair stuffed in the back seat,
He pushes on the funky hand controls

like ski poles,
          guns and brakes,
Slaloms, slides and glides
Along Fred Waring Avenue.

I lean back, floating, flying
          face up to the stars.
Amazed to find
          my able-bodied soul,
                    so unconfined,
                         so free.

January 15, 1989

Waiting for JJ

In the hall
students wait
in the same way I waited
20 years ago
the same hallway
or was it a different one then?
still airless and sterile
no trees have grown up
inside
but paper sprouts in profusion from her door
proclaiming hope and opportunity
for English majors
a safe haven

They tap their feet,
impatient
the black girl, angry, overweight
the young bearded man, resigned
We sit on the ancient couch
covered with a homey, worn-out
bedspread

About to give up
go home
I hear the lilt
of that still strong southern voice
singing its apologies
the tap of her purposeful heels
coming around the corner.

The young man smiles at me.
"You can always hear her coming,"

Then she appears
a little larger than my mind remembers
takes each of us in with
a word, a gesture,
welcoming, including.
I love it that she calls me Liz

April 30, 1993
(rediscovered March 22, 1997 . . . unfinished)

Insomnia

Sleep—
elusive sister—
you escape each night
climbing out my bedroom
window

taking the sheets
off my body
for your ladder
leaving me uncovered,
alone.

There is no cajoling you
to stay
to wrap me
in the warm, unconscious
forgetting
of your mysterious voice,
your thick hair.

Even closed
my eyes stare
like the empty sockets
of the dead.

They hurt with too much vision,
too much light.

August 12, 1992

Untitled

Stepped in dogshit this morning.
On my way to the washing machine
a pile of dirty clothes in my arms
looking for bleach,
my daughter's new white blouse
stained with beer
by some jerk flailing about on a dance floor.
It wasn't her fault.

In the dark, under the house
I slipped slightly, felt the mushy slide
under the soles of my new shoes,
the expletive emerging from my mouth
describing it
perfectly.

It took an entire roll of paper towels, steel wool,
hot water and deodorant spray
to clean it off. The shit got stuck in the grooves
of the soles.

Even now, I'm not quite sure,
imagine myself walking down Main Street
followed by dogs
allured by my scent,
a canine pied piper.

I sit in a quiet cafe, enjoying anonymity.
The young girl at the next table,
who looks like a boy, writes in a checkbook
with a glittery case.
She is reading *The English Patient*.

I want to be reading it too,
to climb into something larger than
this trivial life,
get lost in the desert
find the Cave of the Swimmers
and drown in words
too beautiful for speaking,

as you would climb into a whirlpool bath,
immersed and absorbed,
cleansed beneath the bone.

March 14, 1997

To Smoky

You died today. No one knows why.
You were twelve years old—
not young for a dog.
Still, we were not ready
to say goodbye.

I lit you a candle,
 sang you a song, a chant
        I made up as I went along.
Talked to Lily and Goofy about you—
How you always greeted me
        at the front door
Stood on your hind legs,
        paws on my shoulders
                your face so eager, so dear.

Husky—your breed, your size.
You probably wanted to be pulling an Alaskan sled
        or running free on the tundra,
Instead you lived where it was warm
with people who loved you.

Chained up mostly,
        or in the house,
the result of a youthful indiscretion
        with a goat.
(I always knew you didn't do it—
        just wanted to play.
You were still hoping the goat would wake up
        when they found you.
Didn't even think to hide.)

Now you run through open fields
    no leash, no chain, no rope.
Restored to your Husky essence.
The love of everyone who ever knew you
    powering your endless soul.

January 26, 1999

Two Poems for Lena

There was a very narrow moon
    the night you disappeared—
enough light to see by,
    but not enough to keep from losing you.

The boat awash in water,   suddenly down.
Floating for a moment, you were seen
    clinging to a cushion, holding a red backpack.

What in that instant
    called to you, carried you down—
the lake's embrace more entrancing
    than the lifetime laid out before you?

Your friends floated in a circle,
    calling your name,
      the water teasing them with glimpses
        of your golden hair.

You were gone,
    dissolved like so much sugar in a
      cup of warm water,
        already dreaming your long sleep.

Now the story is told and retold—
    how you were there
and then you weren't.

    Just like your glimmering, perfect
      too-brief life.

II

Over and over I replay the same scene —
    the circle of friends, the new moon,
      the lake, bottomless, haunting

I hear them calling —
    her name falling like stars through
      the earth's atmosphere,
        falling into the lake,
          becoming water.

She has cast off her body
      like clothing she no longer needs.
    She is turning into spirit, into light.

If we are lucky,
    she will come to us in dreams,
      scatter her blossoms among us,
        reminding us never to forget
        this precious instant,
          this warm hand holding your hand.

June 1, 1995

Cello in the Forest

for Toni

Out of its green velvet nest
    you delivered it,
made it welcome
    in our outdoor home,
strings untuned from disuse,
    coaxed into a new harmony
       to play for us.

After the food and the wine
    and the stories
    of our not quite touching yet
       lives,
You held the cello gently
    between your knees,
its hourglass form,
    the shape of the goddess,
drew the bow across a string.

Then my own hand
    held the bow
    drew out a note, and then another. . . .
A scale emerged beneath my fingers —
    a miracle
       of memory
         of hope.

July 20, 1994

Story Circle, Saturday Night

First we eat. The good food
fills our bellies, fills the time before
we are ready to sit in the circle
and set our souls in motion.

I love it when women feed each other.
We eat differently. There is no
main course, no five food groups,
no starch.
Just everything we love.
Ripe nectarines with lemon. Apples
microwaved with cinnamon. Devilled
eggs. A salad with everything in it.
Crusty bread and brie.

Remembering our connections, where we met,
    who we were then. It helps that we
        have someone new to tell it to.

We breathe into a circle.
Candles light our way down to
    another level. Forgotten images swim there,
        lit up like neon fish, suddenly visible.

The stories, like a patchwork, make one
        whole work of art.
There is plenty of time for everyone.
The world disappears, gently,
    leaving only this circle, these voices
        this ring of women.

In the past they would have called us witches,
    burned us at the stake
Tonight we hold the fire in our hands
    witnessing each other's words,
        listening for the truth.

March 26, 1995

My Muse

She lives in the paper,
        swims in the ink of the pen
Hides out in dreams
        where she takes different shapes
Hangs out in coffee shops, writing, writing.

Older than me,
        she feels like my twin
        born from the same spirit egg
Dresses in velvet,
        a hat trimmed with roses,
        quill pen in her loose grasp
Stares down at me
        from my own bookshelf,
        hair tied loosely beneath her hat.

In dreams we dance
        easily together under a warm night sky,
        the stars pulling us into their rhythm.
I find her tucked between
        the leaves of abandoned books.
She finds me sobbing
        in the middle of the night.

No matter how far I travel
        from her loving gaze
                she always calls me back.

February 16, 1998

The Day Before

The day before my birthday
    I awaken early,
      drink coffee in the windowseat,
        write down my dreams.

I am still trying to teach algebra
    to a roomful
      of recalcitrant students.
Even my unconscious can't figure out
    how to fly.

I picture Marcel Marceau
    creating a box with gesture
      imprisoned by
        invisible steel.

Fifty-three years on the planet
    minus one day—
    a year for every card
      plus one . . .

The dwarf woman
    inhabits my dreams
      keeps a flame lit
    melts a candle
      in her wisdom, her innocence.

Meanwhile I rely
    on a mind, a body
      destined for earth like everyone else's.

Temporary quarters.
No matter how much we paint,
  plant flowers, refurbish,
  pretend we will live here forever.

I am more than halfway now.

The wood in the fireplace
  has to burn up
   to do its job.

      July 15, 1996

Gratitude

for Joanne

We lose the trail and find it—
three middle aged couples,
some teenagers, a white dog named Cody,
who herds us along over meadows
of blooming profusion,
across cascading streams,
the melt of a winter so intense that
snow still lingers in August and we throw
snowballs at each other, delighting at the icy thrill,
the chill to the neck.

Slipping and sliding in the slick places,
we trade stories. Like an untrod patch of snow
there is that chance with new friends
to recreate yourself.
Suddenly the blue lake appears, startling.
No fanfare needed,
just the frame of aspen, glint of sun
upon its surface. It would help to remember how
this lake resides always at the heart of things.
Tents pitched by its borders do not change it.

The way back is different. We split off in twos
and the stories go deeper. It is safe here
to be real. You tell your tale of fear and loss
and I tell mine. We are forgiven in each other's company.
No mistake is big enough
to matter for too long. Falling
will not be a sin. Grace catches us by surprise.

August 1995

First Day of School

I wake before dark, picturing their faces,
unknown to me yet still vivid.
The single mothers, punk guys with earrings
and purple hair, older men with tattoos and a past
to live down, sitting in those little desks once again,
nervous. So much depends upon
the first day. Failure haunts my classroom,
makes it hard to try again. To pick up a pen
is a nine foot dive into icy water, an ice-slick
black diamond slope.

The chalk dust conjures a new beginning,
inviting hope. I write on the blackboard.
The words sing out welcome and yes.
The names we call ourselves will be new.
The first day, another chance.

August 16, 1995

After the Break

We sit mute in rows
    awaiting the blow of a question.
Forced to speak in an unfamiliar language,
   having crossed some border in the middle of the night,
     unconscious, asleep,
       dreaming in our native tongue,
        simple syllables.
Now suddenly thrust
  into the harsh academic light—
    the customs officer demanding proof,
    documentation that we belong here
    in the company of gentlemen and scholars.

The forgotten words come grudgingly to the mind,
    as we are asked to define (whose) terms—
      theory, criticism, aphasia—

     Aphasia—yes—
That is the name of the country we have passed through,
 sleeping.
It borrows our words and will not give them back to us
    so easily.
 As with most kidnappings,
    there is a ransom,
   a price to be paid
      for retrieval.

Under the fluorescent light
   in the airless room,
We flinch at the relentless interrogation.

Where is the meadow, the sky,
the sweet flowers we desired
when we came here?

(This poem came out of my experience of going back
to school for my second master's degree. It was published
in the journal *Teaching English in the Two Year College*.)
October 1, 1995

The Change

They told her
    it was all in her head —

these strange volcanic eruptions
    spewing lava over her
        unsleeping body
in the middle of a cold night.

murderous impulses
    gripping her
      weaponless hands

snakes wrapping
      themselves
    around her entrails,
      squeezing the life
        right out of her heart.

Her womb emptied for the last time,
      she traverses the pathless wood,
    hearing the faint voices
      of other lost ones,
        searching for a way out.

The breadcrumb trail to childhood
  long since eaten,
    the witch hidden
      in the trees
    becomes her aspiration,
      her deliverance.

August 10, 1992

not permanent

She assured me it was not
permanent—the silver ring
suddenly stuck
in the middle of her tongue
flashing quickly, glinting
in the dim restaurant light like
a fish sliding beneath the surface,
a jewel hidden
in the folds of a flower.

My stomach flipped over,
the room spun around.

She had allowed this to happen,
wanted it inside her mouth
a silver secret
anchored in the body,
something to feel to know you were
alive—is that it?—
pierced to become whole.

We talk.
I try to understand,
try not to pass out, hurl
my food across the room,
picturing her, my baby girl
her tongue in someone else's mouth
or his tongue touching
the little silver ball
a new source of pleasure
she has had the nerve
to buy.

Almost invisible
not for decoration
like an earring or even—
God forbid—
a nose ring,
a more bizarre, perverted,
private thing.

Cold ball bearing,
mercury come loose
from the thermometer—

It doesn't matter if it makes me dizzy,
if my eyes roll back
in my head—

The silver ball
in the center of her tongue
strikes its singular note
fills the air with
a strange new music, hers.

March 18, 1996

Bessie Smith Dies Again

In my dream she is alive.
A middle class black woman
with straightened hair
surrounded by books,
her name changed to protect
her privacy.
Not as old as you would think.

She agrees to a picture.
Doesn't want to be in front.

You been a good ol' wagon,
But you done broke down.

I can't believe
no one knows she's here.
My secret treasure
waiting to be mined.
Pull out my tape recorder,
steno pad, all my good questions.

25 cents? No, no!
I ain't payin' 25 cents to get in nowhere

I want to know
about the parties, the booze, the men,
how it felt to sing
in the sweat of those jook joints
when you didn't know where you would
sleep or if . . .

Woke up this mornin'
with an awful achin' head

And how did you die, really?
Did you bleed to death
your blood running black
through a white world?

That's when I know
I'm dreaming.
Bessie is dead
already, her life laid out
in those scratchy records
that already contain
all her answers.

July 14, 1996

For Joan Brown

(1938–1990)

In the beginning
    you only knew
you had to paint

Troweling it on
    with housepaint brushes
        from gallon cans
    layer upon layer
        of rich, glorious pigment
    like frosting you could lick off the spoon.

You said it was an attitude,
    this enormous energy—
    paint bleeding to the floor
        female, fecund
You laughed at the juiciness of it,
    refused to make your paintings smaller

Images coming so fast
    you couldn't stop
You painted everything there was to see
    your child
        the refrigerator
            Bob the dog
    husbands two and three

And the invisible fears—
    the rats, the mice
        sculpted of wire and fur
    the nightmare swim in the bay,
        the sharks

All the old terrors
      thrown up on canvas
            six feet tall

The air swims with fish, cats, dogs, birds,
            Egyptian hieroglyphics
Dancers and swimmers
      lovers and sinners and

You at the center of each painting
Your eyes two blazing turquoise
Refusing to blink.
Portraits of the soul
      in search of itself.

The soft oval of your face
      evoking   Anais—
            your diaries in paint

I picture you, barely five feet tall
      standing on a ladder
            to reach high enough
      to touch your vision.

Standing on a ladder
            the day you died.
Installing an obelisk in an Indian shrine.

Did you see the turret break loose,
      point itself straight at you—
            a guided missile
                  your fifth husband
                        your destiny?

                        January 10, 1999

The World is Always Alive

And everything in it has a name.
Here in the desert's stark terrain
The ocotillo blooms fiery red
Bushes of desert encelia
soften the rockface
with yellow abundance.
As we climb towards
the chaparral.
life bursts from every crevice.

Pay attention, each cactus says,
to me—spiky, upright, fleshy,
unique.

Altitude is the gate
to these communities,
secret code of
exclusion.

Cholla cactus
does not grow
with lupine, sagebrush
    scrub oak, pines.

In the grove of juniper and pinyon pine
a lizard keeps watch
atop a rock
knowing we are mere tourists
and will soon be gone.

April 29, 1998

Lingering at the Doorstep

They are saying goodbye
     against a night glittery with cold
     the moon a frozen smile
     frost already forming on the sides
       and tops of things

The warmth of the kitchen at her back
     making a muted appeal
     to rewind time.

She leans carefully into the leather of his coat
     reaches up to stroke his cheek.

When did his smooth skin turn to sandpaper?
     his voice slide from soprano into bass?
   How can it be that he is gazing down at her?

The only thing the same is that she worries.

They talk of this and that,
     of nothing.
His gloved hand on her shoulder,
     weighty, reassuring.

She is so aware
     of his motorcycle waiting,
     of the scent of a cologne she didn't choose,
     of the women she hasn't met and won't.

Still will any ever know what she has known—
the fierce intimacy
of those brief moments
at her breast.

January 10, 1999

Birthday Girl

This morning I woke
    to the absence of you
        in the room where you were born,
    the day already half spent
      where you are now,
          surrounded by strangers.

You are only
   the most important
     being on the planet,
only the reason
    for any of it.

I, the container
    that once held you briefly
       on your journey to earth.

It is not for the tree to say
    what becomes of the fruit,
Not for the seed to know
    who picks the flower.

You leave your teens behind
    like the shoes left scattered
       on your bedroom floor,
Greet the evening
    while we still grope in morning darkness,
Learn to speak a new language
    as once you absorbed
       your mother tongue.

Brave girl
  your sweet adventure
    stretched before you.

Even if I could,
  I wouldn't call you back.

      August 28, 1997

January, Vista Trail

They paved this road along the cliff for wheelchairs,
put in picnic tables too,
each on smooth cement,
a wide lip at either end to slide the chair beneath.
Today it works for two black dogs, leash-free,
and me.

The road up here, washed out twice
along the edge in the last rains,
turning two lanes into one,
discourages drivers,
leaves us alone
on the rim of the continent.

The dogs entertain themselves
with the smells of their predecessors—
invisible monuments to pioneer canines.
They wander in sometimes intersecting circles,
        never far away,
like self-sufficient toddlers.

To the south,   a smooth expanse
  of hazy blue ocean, dappled with rocks,
        white fringe of foam outlining the land.

My mind is as blank as the sky
        and as full of clouds.
They look like chalkdust smeared
        against a blackboard.
Another year presents itself.

The smooth clean surface I used to see
now looks already cluttered
        like the sky holding its burden of clouds.

A hawk glides, dips low.
My dog, forever hopeful
        runs up the hill full tilt
        as if he's never chased a bird before
                and lost.

Horizons are by definition
        out of reach.
Still I will always walk
        to the edge of any landscape.

                                                January 9, 1997

Hale-Bopp '97

Driving home I glimpsed it
    out my windshield—
        almost ran
    the car off the road
            keeping it in sight

Glowing ball
    tail flowing
 ice and dirt they say
      but you couldn't prove it
         by me
This far away
    it's fairy dust and magic
       a rorschach of childish dreams

No surprise
    39 people hypnotized themselves
        to death
        thinking to catch a spaceship out
            of here
                behind its light.

* * * * * * * * *

Next night driving home
    again it appears.
This time I have someone
    to share it with.
We drive to a hillside
    away from city lights
Stand in the cold air
    till our breath copies the comet's tail

Watching it seem to stand still in space
        just as we too seem to stand still. . . .

                    * * * * * * * * *

For a few weeks
        the whole world watches
    the same beam of light.

No matter how poor you are
        you can see it.
No telescope,
        TV, computer,
    or ability to read required.

I think of Kurdish tribesmen,
        African children,
                farmers in Nebraska
    prisoners at San Quentin

all looking up.

                    * * * * * * * * *

Sitting in Richard's living room
        waiting for Maria to show up

She calls collect
        car pulled over to the side of the road
Tells us to go outside and look —
                Look!   at the comet

We walk up the hill
　　　shielding our eyes from the streetlamp
This time it blazes in the Cazadero sky.

Even in the daytime, I think,
　　　It's still there.

* * * * * * * * *

I picture the comet shrouded in sunlight
　　　waiting in the wings
　　　　　emerging each night for its limited run
　　　to rave reviews.
The days fill up with errands
　　　and paper.
Still the comet
　　　calls to me
　　　　　each night
　　　reminding me
　　　　　　to look up.

April 1, 1997

Dear Billy

for Billy Collins

I had to write and tell you
I got your poem
driving down Highway 101
through the Central Valley.
It reached me in San Luis Obispo
where we stopped for coffee.

Somewhere outside Salinas
your voice was on the radio
reading "Osso Bucco"
and I craved more of your poems
the way sometimes just the thought
of cinnamon buns
propels you to a bakery,
the memory of sugary icing melting
in your mouth

In Barnes and Noble
I found *The Art of Drowning*
with the baying dog
on the cover, your picture
in the back, and my new friend,
"Osso Bucco" in the Table of Contents.
I was glad to be in a strange town
where no one I knew would see me
buying your book at a chain store.

We got our lattes to go
and took you with us down the highway,
my husband driving so I could read to him.

The first poem — "Dear Reader" —
the beginning
of our correspondence
old friend, chance acquaintance.

Your words
will always carry with them
this moving landscape —
the emerald breasts of hills
sloping toward the sea,
a sky filling with cumulus wonder,
large trucks passing each other
on the curving, shimmering expanse of road,
Keith Jarrett's "You Don't Know What Love Is,"
and the sound of your voice
becoming my voice
writer and reader merging
in their inevitable unplanned rendezvous.

It is possible that you will not like this response.
Perhaps you will regret
having spawned more bad poetry.
Maybe you had hoped
your Reader would stay
in her place, the grateful recipient
of your words.

But tonight she was dragged
into this motel bathroom,
stripped of her pride
and forced at penpoint
to sit on the cold floor
and write of this simple miracle —

how poetry can drop suddenly
into your life
and change everything.

February 6, 1999

Waiting for the Muse

On hold. Musak playing in the background.
Calls will be answered in the order
in which they are received. To ensure quality control,
some calls may be monitored.
Stay on the line. Stay on
the line. Queued up, waiting
my turn for inspiration.
What will it take? A fluke, a joke, a heartache.
Sequestered inside my self-created
cell, wearing an orange jumpsuit, awaiting
the call. Will I be given a hearing, a warning,
an airing, a blessing, a smile?
Plucking the petals from an oracular daisy,
I ask about love, about grace.
Meanwhile I hold the receiver,
Listening, always listening for directions.

May 31, 1995

Making Art with Cheryl

for Cheryl King

She spreads the bright paper
　　before us, gives us tools,
　　demonstrates how easy it might be
　　　　to allow
the images that sing in our midnight dreams
　　to live in the material world.

With exacto knife and gluestick,
　　chopstick and stencil pressed against a windowpane,
she shows us how a card is born—
　　a gift midwifed from soul to paper
　　　　by your own hand.

She floats nearby, encouraging,
　　　　while I fight back
my urge to leave,
　　to throw down the scissors and the paste,
　　　　the sponges and the styrofoam.

Why try? It's always a mess.
　　I can't find where to make the fold,
　　　　hold the knife upside down,
　　　　　　smudge the card with paint.
　　Panicky, watch beauty
　　　　sprouting quickly all around me.

I breathe,
　　let in the music,
　　　　allow myself another chance.
Pat helps me fold the paper, use the knife.
Diane shows me how to wet the sponge.

Cheryl knows just when to put
        her soft hand on my shoulder,
                when to tell me I am doing fine.

I think of my students,
    of what it takes to try again to write,
        despite the red-inked
                years of having failed,
            what courage they must daily gather
                just to show up.

The music softens, and
        we rush to bring our projects to a close.
    surprised by the grace
                of her farewell gift—

a piece of her own art,
        for each of us—
                an image to remind us
                of the artist's heart,
                    the open hand,
        the holy work of teaching.

June 14, 1997

Transformation, Trying Again

Why does it take so long
    and why does it seem like the same game
    played over and over
    on a circular board
    the awarenesses piling up behind me
    but no release
    stuck this time on the mental plane
        remembering other games
            the illusion of progress
                of moving forward
I am always working on the same thing
    wanting my life back
        the only one I have
        and who could have taken it from me
        if I hadn't cooperated
        an internal fifth column, constantly betraying
        giving me over to the enemy.
Yet the reclamation is a massive job
    requiring a team of experts,
    perhaps a guard
    to walk beside me, slap down my hand
    when I reach for another task, a TV dial,
    a glass of wine, a magazine
This feels too punitive
    not transformation but prohibition.
The crescent moon smiles high above
    my loft window.
She doesn't have these problems
    doesn't go in for self-torture
        in the middle of the night
The mermaid made of leaded glass
    keeps looking out to sea

The waves thunder their endless greeting
to the shore
Why do I think my cycles will be any less
repetitive?

November 19, 1995

Anniversary of an Earthquake

This time the earthquake is farther away—
    Japan—Kobe
        not L.A.
At home the rift is widening,
    the edges beginning to fray.
The brown spots keep reappearing on the rug,
    the damp odor of his disapproval lingers
After she has cleaned up the kitchen
    and made up the beds,
And when she steps outside into the cool mist of morning,
A skunk has filled the empty air with its perfume.

What is it this time?
He won't say. Only that his back hurts.
They are in for it again.
June Cleaver in the morning kitchen never can make up
    for the sleepless night before,
        the dinner uncooked,
            the eyes that dare to look
                away.

Dancing for twenty years, they still don't quite
    glide.
 She thinks she is following well
   until she notices her neck hurts, cramped against his
 shoulder, or she steps on his
        toes.

She dreams of Kobe—the hole in the earth—
    as a hole in a tooth, belonging to someone else—
      a cousin to herself.

He walks away, holding tight
        to a briefcase full of importance.
She is left alone in a kitchen
        reeking of absence.

January 25, 1995

Chance Encounter

While picking out our evening meal,
delighting in the joy of
a dinner for two on vacation, suddenly
you saw her—
the ex-wife of your once-best-friend—
came and got me near the garlic, panicky—

We didn't want to see her,
didn't want to have to talk, to know
how she had aged alone,
her face pinched and puffy,
contracted in upon itself,

her mouth with no one to talk to
no one to kiss,
hands with no hand to stroke,
grasping the packaged food.

Averting our eyes, we yanked our frozen yogurt
   from the freezer
       and escaped,
     dodging her ghost
         back there, waiting

two fugitive survivors
     shaking,
        wondering why

July 18, 1995

Home Mom

Now that you are grown
I am finally
what you always wanted —
a home mom.

I plan meals,
shop and cook,
watch daytime TV
and keep your room neat.
It's easy without you
in it.

But where did you go
little girl?
Why couldn't you wait for me
to realize
that milk and cookies at 3:00
would be so much better
than a meeting?

I watch the school bus
ride our road
and listen for your
steps on the walkway

wanting to hear
all about your day.

May 6, 1999

To Grandma at 90

I am looking up at you
As if you had climbed a tall mountain
Your tiny form waving to me from the top
Your voice, still strong, calling to me
To keep coming.

You have always lived looking up,
Have taken every turn of the trail
With faith in your own firm step
And the ways in which God provides strength
When it is needed.

You have survived so much,
Including the ways in which
I have disappointed you.

I have not always brought you nachas —
And yet, never have I been without your love.

You have taught me what it means
To love without condition,
To accept what can't be changed,
And to find beauty, even
Along the rockiest of paths.

I see your chin set firm as your walk,
Strong and determined,
Looking up at us — We.
Who were once your babies,
All taller than you now,
Stooping to hear your wisdom,

Catch your laughter,
See the world as only you can show it to us
From where you stand.

II

"We should only have our health"
You would say
When I was a child growing up
With the smell of your chicken soup in the air,
And the Sabbath challah shining on the table,
Your fingers framing the candles,
Whispering your prayers for the family
Into the flames.

I didn't understand then.
I thought that health was something
Everyone had,
Like food or clothing
Or a bed to sleep in.

I never understood
Why you said "please God"
Whenever you talked about the future,
Or what "kine-ahorah" meant
When you praised a child's beauty.

I didn't know
That there could be loss or pain or death
Or that people grow old.
Wrapped in the warmth and safety
Of our home,
The ritual of Friday night,
The holidays unfolding the year
Like a bright ribbon,

The rhythmic pattern of feasts
And solemn days,
I was safe inside my childhood.

One day I realized you were getting older.
Alice said, "Don't take so many baths, Grandma,
So you won't shrink,"
And we all laughed.

But something was different.
I began to understand
That you would not always be with me
And about health
And how it might not always be with me.

I began to feel how precious indeed
Was the life I had taken for granted
And the lives of those I loved.

"We should only have our health,"
You would say,
And I am beginning to understand
The daily miracle
Of being alive.

How health makes all things possible.
This gathering of our family,
The harvest of your ninety years
Shining in the center of our celebration
Like the Sabbath candles,
Your long life, a blessing
You have earned.
And the work left by your hands,
Your love made visible,

Glowing
In each of us.

With love and admiration, Elizabeth — October 10, 1976

Family

You were with him
    at the end
All of you
    Breathing his last breaths
    with him and for him
Releasing him
    from blood and bone and pain
    into pure spirit
    light and free as air
He knew
    your touch
    your reverential care
He felt it all
You gave back everything
    he'd given
Loved him through
    the doors of death
Together
Holding one another's hands against
    the emptiness
This must be the meaning of it all
To be there
    at the beginning
    at the end
A family.

Dayle, Sr.

Always I will remember him,
Standing in the corner by the sink,
Jingling the change in his pocket,
The ice in his drink.
A twinkle in his eye
As he reached
For another cigarette.
The five dollar bill stuffed in each
Grandchild's pocket
To be revealed later
Too late to be returned.
So handsome he was always,
The shock of white hair
Above a face a little too ruddy,
Taller than any of his sons,
Quiet with the force of a volcano,
Dormant.

There was little we could talk about.
On politics we always disagreed,
And I don't know much about golf or football.
Yet from the moment I first
Walked into his home —
The frizzy-haired radical divorcé
Who'd caused his son to live in sin —
He always made me welcome,
Took me in,
And made me know he loved me,
That somehow I belonged.
This gracious man
With greater dignity than I may ever see again.

Your spirit floats away now,
Hovering over the body it no longer needs.
I will never forget you,
        Or your special gifts of grace.
Always I will remember you.

April 19, 1988

Friday Night Alone

All day I wandered the world,
    groping for where I belonged,
        not fitting in anywhere.

Lunch in the sun,
    everyone talking.
  Words felt foreign, as if I were
        a tourist among natives.
  Tears filled my throat.
    I couldn't swallow.
  It seemed as though my heart
     was turning black and purple in front of everybody.
       I couldn't get home fast enough.

"What's the matter, Mom, are you OK?"
She sits in my lap, too big for me to hold
   and lets me cry into her hair.

"It's nothing," I say. "It's everything.
    I'm getting old
  and nothing I've ever done (except you)
  seems to amount to anything at all."

   The cat sleeps at my side,
     the night catches my breath.
I wish for the phone to ring,
   for my insides to stop holding on.

My pen is a breathing tube,
     keeping me alive.

                     March 24, 1995

Buried Alive

When they removed
the stone from the door
    she emerged again into the light,
        through the crawl space,
           the trap door.

Interred for so long,
    she had forgotten
        the kiss of the sun
           on her weathered cheek,
    the smell of rain-soaked earth
        the cry of birds, escaping north.

They treated her body very gently,
    handling it as they would
        the flesh and bones of someone newborn.

She tries to understand—
    the earth seeped so far into her skin,
        her blood clogged within her arteries,
      her face like desert roads
      no oasis.

Their voices scatter around her
    like broken shards of pottery.
Her parched syllables will not form
    themselves into words.
Her arms flap helplessly
      about her frame

It is no use
　　to try to prove she lives.

May 11, 1994

Storms of '98

It's all over TV —
rivers flooding, people forced out of their homes,
freeways blocked, traffic snarled.

A hillside moves in Rio Nido,
nests built on its higher ground
collapsing beneath its slide,
people moved into shelters
in the middle of the night.
Some in shock, some grieving,
some angry with the bearer of bad news,
the bureaucrat, announcing
"You may not be able to go home for months, if then."

"What am I supposed to do?
I have kids to get to school, a job I have to get to!"
Suddenly homeless, this man who was barely
making it rails against another mortal
when it is so much bigger.
Too much water at once,
pulling down mountains,
rearranging the human landscape.

You can't live in your home
like I can't live in my body,
forced out by multiplying cells.
What am I supposed to do? I scream
to no one in particular.
I have a life I need to live!

But the mountain is moving
and it hasn't stopped yet.

February 9, 1998

What is Left Behind

I face the dark mountain
    coming up out of a long valley
        through feeling fields, whatwheat
            questiongrass
alive to   birdfeathers
    fluttering softly
against a window
        of nothing but violet sky

What coincides with the bribe I made myself
    for I know I made myself a bribe
        handed quickly under the table
          from right to left
    but the hands knew what they were doing
      and I knew

I am terrified to leave anything out—
    the small places where I loved to hide
    the tiny bedrooms with their sloping roofs
I could contain all of me then
    within that slanted space

Everything important happened there.

When I die
    will all these die with me?
the tears shed over the wrong people, the right people,
    the gold that shines in the trees in the twilight,
   Jones Beach in winter, freezing wind and snow on sand,
    my baby's skin against mine, her fine hair
      nuzzling my neck

the labyrinth of my thoughts, their pattern
undecipherable

A universe in every moment,
        every breath
            the interior of
                this single human life
        unable to be passed down, touched or seen

the awful absence
            behind the absence

June 25, 1999

An Atheist Prays

These days
I find myself talking to God,
asking for help, for strength.
It doesn't seem to matter
that I don't know who I'm talking to.
I keep on anyway
just the way I keep
getting up in the morning
even though I know there will be
more bad news
and my body feels like a strange
drafty hallway
I don't quite inhabit.

Still I put one foot and then the other on the floor,
make my way slowly and desperately
through the day
holding onto whatever I can grasp
for balance.
Sometimes it is the word "please"
sometimes "thank you."
I remember each small precious moment—
the feel of the bow
moving across the cello
the way the woman who took my blood
smiled her encouragement,
my husband's soft eyes
loving me no matter what.

Sometimes my life seems
like Barstow in a heatwave
and me an illegal, locked

in an airless truck.
Other times it is verdant green,
Yosemite in spring,
waterfalls everywhere.
I just can't seem
to get enough of it.

I keep on talking to someone,
grateful but greedy.

June 30, 1998

How can we know the dancer
from the dance?

William Butler Yeats

ELIZABETH CARLSON was born in Brooklyn, New York, on July 16, 1943. Her father was a research physicist at Brooklyn Polytechnic College, and her mother was a high school speech pathologist. When Elizabeth was twelve years old, her family moved with the postwar housing migration to Levittown, Long Island, where she and her younger sister were raised. From childhood, Elizabeth loved the written word. She wrote many stories with her friends, and she wrote poetry.

Elizabeth attended Brandeis University for a year and then enrolled at the University of California, Berkeley. She actively participated in the Free Speech Movement and often recalled that one of her proudest moments was her arrest during the Sproul Hall sit-in. That arrest was symbolic of her lifelong commitment to human rights and individual freedom. Elizabeth graduated from the University of California with a degree in English, awarded with highest honors.

After college, Elizabeth began teaching English at Berkeley High School. Recognizing the need to nurture the development of students who were not excelling in the traditional high school structure, she helped create Berkeley High's "Community High School," an alternative school within a school. The creation of Community High, an innovative answer to a difficult question, is one example of Elizabeth's contributions during her thirty years of work in education and human services.

In 1971, Elizabeth moved to Sonoma County in northern California and entered Sonoma State University, where she earned a master's degree in psychology. Her master's thesis, an expanded journal describing her journey and evolution as a woman, was published in book form. Anaïs Nin contributed to the cover notes of *To Deliver Me of My Dreams*, which was widely read in Women's Studies programs throughout the United States and Canada. After completing her degree, Elizabeth helped found a community counseling center in Sonoma County, dedicated to helping people with personal, relationship, and family problems.

Elizabeth returned to education when she was selected to help develop the first program for students with disabilities at Santa Rosa Junior College. The program, now an educational model in the state of California, remains a monument to Elizabeth's creativity and commitment to helping individuals realize their full potential.

Throughout her career as teacher, counselor, and program director, Elizabeth continued to write poetry. Writing led her back to school. During a sabbatical leave in 1995, Elizabeth returned to Sonoma State University, where she completed a second master's degree, this time in English. Her thesis, "Ordinary Words," was a compilation and critical analysis of her own poetry. The work done in that year forms the basis for this collection.

Returning to her work at Santa Rosa Junior College, Elizabeth became the Assistant Dean of Arts, Culture, and Communication. Shortly after assuming that position, in the fall of 1997, she was diagnosed with cancer. She died on January 13, 2000.

Throughout her long illness, Elizabeth continued to write poetry and meet with her many friends with whom she shared a passion for literature, art, dance, music, and the creative process. She helped plan the publication of this collection; the final production was completed by her friends.